# This book belongs to

Maisie
─────────────────────────

Monty the Camel wants to be a Race Horse.

Copyright 2020 Robert Kay.

All rights reserved.

No part of this publication may be reproduced, distributed, or transmitted in any form or by any means, including photocopying, recording, or other electronic or mechanical methods, without prior permission of the author.

Illustrations and design by Zoe Mellors

ISBN: 979-8-8763-7253-6

First edition 2024

# MONTY
## the Camel wants to be a
# RACE HORSE

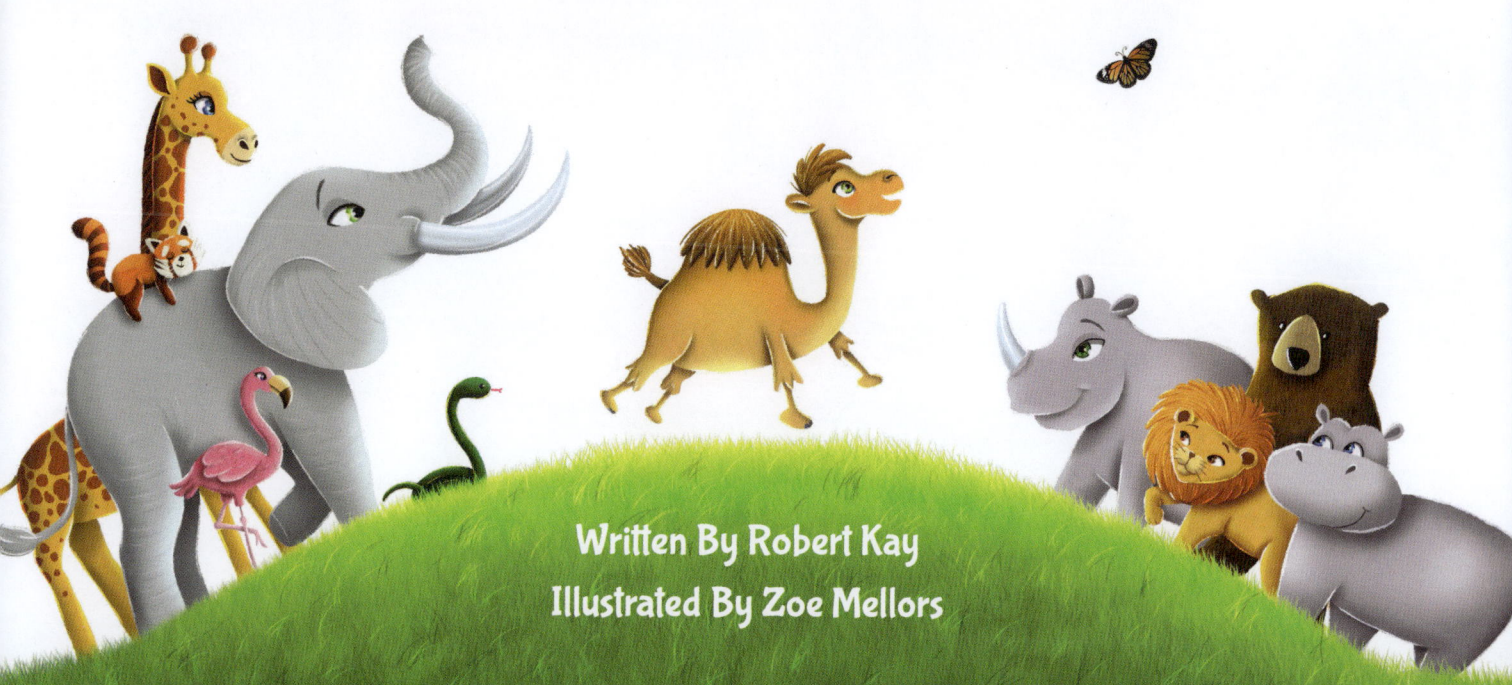

Written By Robert Kay
Illustrated By Zoe Mellors

Monty was a camel, of course he was a mammal.
He dreamt of being a horse, which we know he is not....... of course.
We'll start from the start
Because as we know the start is the important part

When Monty was born, he was born in a zoo
A zoo in England, a zoo we have all been to
Now this zoo overlooked a grand race course
This is when Monty saw the most magnificent race horse

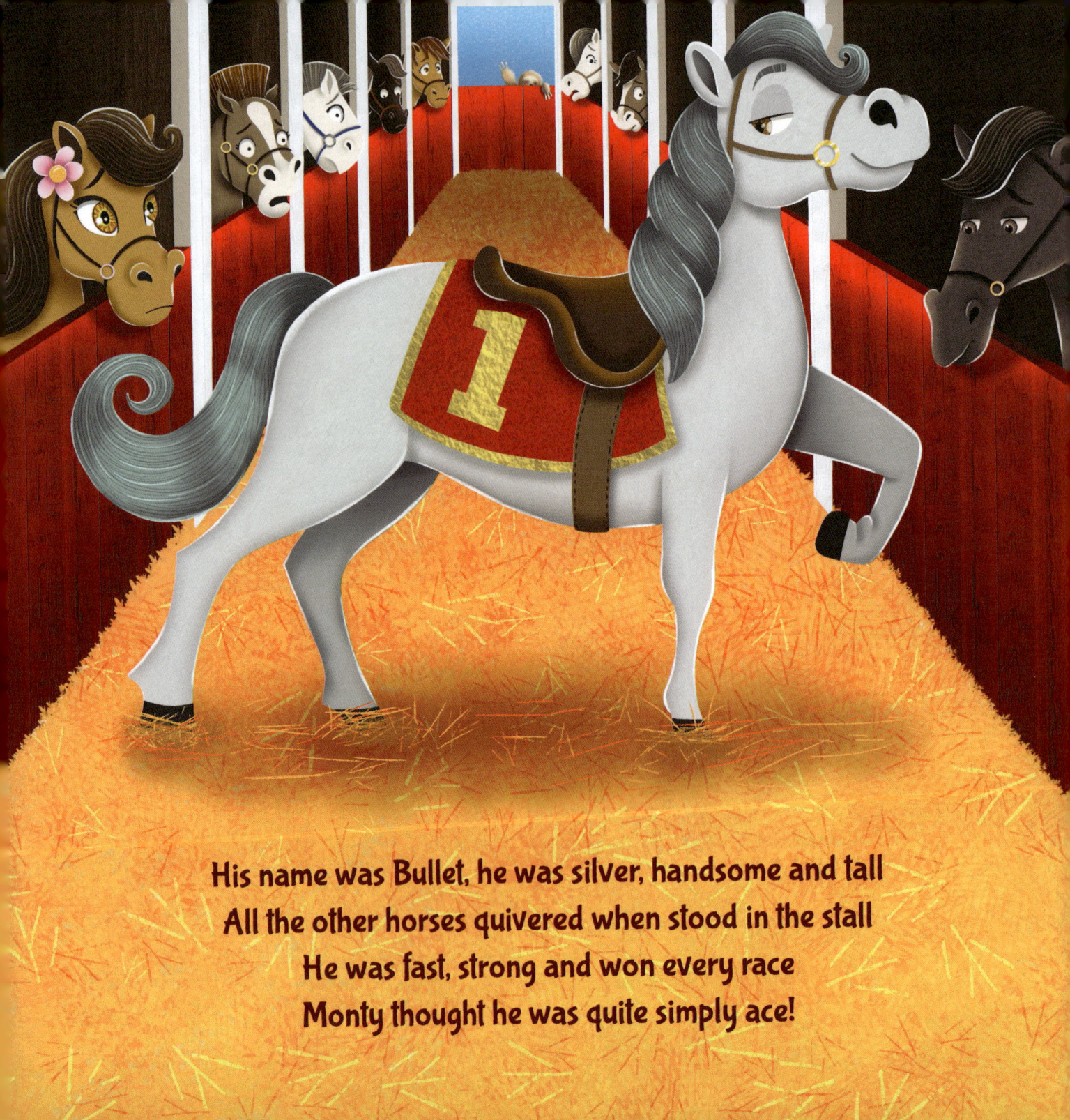

His name was Bullet, he was silver, handsome and tall
All the other horses quivered when stood in the stall
He was fast, strong and won every race
Monty thought he was quite simply ace!

Monty then had the most amazing idea
He thought his idea was the idea of the year
This is what I'm going to do
I'll hold a running race at the zoo

Straight away Monty ran as fast as he could
To tell his parents and jumping over mud
Mum and Dad I want to race today
We need to get all the animals to race straight away

His dad chuckled. Today? You've not got a chance
Today is the annual zoo tango dance
Monty then asked if they could have the race soon
His dad thought and replied, after the next full moon

That will be the 3rd of September!
With a big grin Monty agreed, that's the day to remember.
Today was the August the 31st
Monty thought waiting was quite simply the worst!
But as the day grew closer
Monty put up a poster

Race day arrived and Monty was ready to go
He was feeling fast fast fast, not slow slow slow
The animals all lined up waiting to set off
Animals of all sizes, even a sloth!

They all dashed off from the starting line
Monty was in front running past the toilet sign
They jumped over the rose flower beds
Where the two lions stopped to rest their lazy heads

Next, past the baboon house, and past the lake
When the hippo stopped and jumped in to take a break

The race was in full flow and the crowd shouted with glee
All of a sudden the giraffe stopped to eat from her favourite tree

The polar bear stopped at the very next jump
To scratch his back on a large tree stump
Monty ran on unaware no one else was in the race
He looked behind, saw no one was running and tears ran down his face

As quick as a flash Monty decided to run away
He was so sad he ran to the race course to stay
Monty arrived ready to race with Bullet and the rest
This would prove that he was the best

He asked the horses if they wanted to race at the zoo
The horses replied, racing is serious and we're not racing you
Camels cannot race horses and win
They ran round Monty, making his head spin

The horses ran off, laughing all the way
This made Monty sadder than earlier that very same day
Monty was now so sad, he felt so alone
He wanted to see his Mum and Dad, so decided to go home

When he got home he told his Mum what the horses did
He then ran to his room, under his quilt and hid
The next day after, the zoo was back to being what a zoo should be
Lions sleeping, monkeys swinging, wallabies jumping happily

Monty stood and smiled, saying I'm a camel
And a camel is the best mammal
I'm strong, handsome and tall
My Mum and Dad love me and that's the best of all

The animals then decided that every year they would hold the zoo race
Called the sleeping, swimming, eating, jumping race

It doesn't matter what position they come
The important thing is that they all have fun

# About the Author

Alongside the amazingly talented Zoe Mellors, this is the second book they have published together.

The beautiful illustrations and heartfelt characters, Robert aims to encourage children to feel good about who they are and wants to help them to grow, thrive become confident in all they do.

Robert's inspiration comes from his two young children, their innocence and their wonderful imagination.

He loves writing books and spending time with his wife, two children, making memories and of course going to the zoo.

# Other Books By Robert Kay

Poppy the cow, innocently watching the world go by, decides it is time to figure out what happens to her milk and who takes it and why. She sets out on a mission to find out. With the help of her friends on the farm, Poppy hopes to find answers.

Will Poppy find out who the milk thief is?

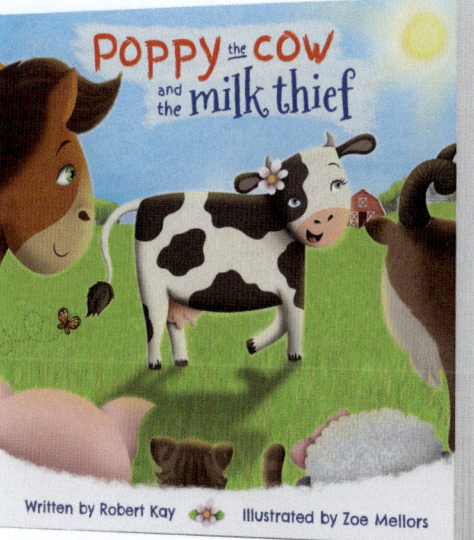

Printed in Great Britain
by Amazon